The Branches of the U.S. GOVERNMENT

Terence M. Stanton

New York

Published in 2009 by The Rosen Publishing Group, Inc.
29 East 21st Street, New York, NY 10010

Book Design: Michael J. Flynn

Photo Credits: Cover (White House) © James Steidl/Shutterstock; cover (U.S. Capitol) © Cristina Ciochina/
Shutterstock; cover (U.S. Supreme Court) © Jonathan Larsen/Shutterstock; p. 4 © Monkey Business Images/
Shutterstock; p. 6 © MPI/Hulton Archive/Getty Images; p. 9 © Paul J. Richards/AFP/Getty Images;
p. 11 © Saul Loeb/AFP/Getty Images; p. 12 © Joe Raedle/Getty Images; p. 14 (flags) © Carsten Reisinger/
Shutterstock; p. 17 (top) © rebvt/Shutterstock; p. 17 (middle) © Steve Rosset/Shutterstock; p. 17 (bottom) ©
Anthony Berenyi/Shutterstock; p. 18 © Justin Sullivan/Getty Images; p. 21 © Getty Images; p. 22 ©
Adam Lohr/Shutterstock; p. 25 © Robert Nickelsberg/Getty Images; p. 27 © Pat Semansky/Getty Images;
p. 29 © Amy Walters/Shutterstock; p. 30 © Miodrag Gajic/Shutterstock.

ISBN: 978-1-4358-0173-8
6-pack ISBN: 978-1-4358-0174-5

Manufactured in the United States of America

Contents

Teamwork

Do you and your classmates have responsibilities in your classroom? Does your teacher give each student a different job? One of your classmates might be chosen to wash the chalkboard at the end of a school day. Another might be in charge of taking attendance in the morning. A third person might turn off the lights when your class leaves the room. What other tasks need to be done around your classroom? What would happen if two students argued over who turns off the lights and who takes attendance? There would be confusion and the classroom wouldn't run well. When everyone

knows their role, we can work together as a team. This helps to reduce problems.

In many ways, good government works like a good classroom. The U.S. government is divided into federal, state, and local governments. Each level is separated into three parts, or "branches." Each branch has its own role to accomplish. If one branch tries to do the job of another branch, problems may arise. The branches need to work together as a team.

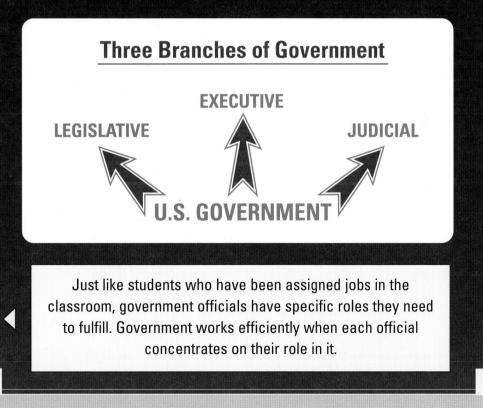

Just like students who have been assigned jobs in the classroom, government officials have specific roles they need to fulfill. Government works efficiently when each official concentrates on their role in it.

Scene at the Signing of the Constitution of the United States by H. C. Christy, 1940

The Federal Government

The founding fathers of the United States set the rules for U.S. government when they wrote the **U.S. Constitution**. They had two main problems they wanted to avoid. First, they wanted to avoid creating a government like the British **monarchy** from which they had just won their independence by winning the American Revolution. Second, they wanted to avoid the weaknesses of the **Articles of Confederation**, which was the document of laws that governed the United States before the Constitution was created. The Articles of Confederation gave the federal government less power than state governments. How was the young nation going to avoid having a government that was too strong or too weak?

America's founding fathers came up with a system of checks and balances. This means that each branch of government is limited in what it can do by the other two branches. Each branch can "check" the power of the other branches. The power is "balanced" between all three branches. The division of responsibilities among

Between 1937 and 1939, Congress discussed having a painting made to celebrate the 150th anniversary of the signing of the U.S. Constitution. H.C. Christy finished his painting in 1940. Today the painting hangs in the east grand stairway of the U.S. Capitol.

the three branches of the federal government is known as the separation of powers.

The Legislative Branch of the Federal Government

The **legislative** branch of the federal government is called Congress. The main power of Congress is the ability to make laws. Article I of the Constitution grants the legislative branch its power. That article also states that Congress will have two houses, or parts: the Senate and the House of **Representatives**. Voters in each state elect their senators and representatives (the members of the House). Each senator serves a term of 6 years. Each representative serves a 2-year term. Each state has two senators. Since there are fifty states, there are 100 senators. A state's number of representatives is based on its population. States with larger populations have more representatives. In 2008, the House had 435 members.

One of the major checks that Congress has on the president's power is the ability to override, or set aside, a veto. A veto is the

Congress, shown here, has other important responsibilities, too. For example, they have the power to declare war on another nation. ▶

president's way of saying no to a law Congress wants to make. However, Congress can override a veto if two-thirds of its members vote against the president's decision. This is an example of checks and balances at work.

The Executive Branch of the Federal Government

The president of the United States heads the **executive** branch of the government. The president is also called the commander in chief because he's the leader of the military. The president is elected by the people to serve a 4-year term and can only be re-elected once. This was not always the case. A limit on the number of terms the president can serve became part of the Constitution in 1951 with the addition of the Twenty-Second Amendment. This is another check placed on the power of the executive branch.

The president's most important duty is to enforce the laws created by Congress. He can also place a check on Congress's ability to make laws. The president might disagree with a proposed law known as a bill that Congress sends to him for approval. The president can veto this bill if he believes it's not in the nation's best interests. The president serves as our representative around the world, too. He often meets with leaders of other nations to discuss issues that are important to all countries.

The Seal of the President of the United States has changed since it was first used by President Rutherford D. Hayes in 1880. This is what the seal looks like today.

Did You Know?

If the president dies, becomes unable to perform his duties, resigns, or is removed from office, the Constitution allows for the vice president to become president. The Constitution doesn't say who comes next in line. Congress set up the following order:

1. vice president
2. speaker of the House of Representatives
3. president pro tempore of the Senate
4. secretary of state
5. secretary of the treasury
6. secretary of defense
7. attorney general
8. secretary of the interior
9. secretary of agriculture
10. secretary of commerce
11. secretary of labor
12. secretary of health and human services
13. secretary of housing and urban development
14. secretary of transportation
15. secretary of energy
16. secretary of education
17. secretary of veterans affairs

The Judicial Branch of the Federal Government

The U.S. court system makes up the **judicial** branch of our federal government. The most powerful court in the United States—the Supreme Court—was established by Article III of the Constitution. The Supreme Court has nine members and is led by a chief justice, or judge. The members of the Supreme Court are not elected. They're appointed by the president and approved by the Senate. This is another way that the branches of government check

John Roberts Jr., shown here with his wife, Jane Sullivan, and Justice John Paul Stevens, is the current chief justice of the Supreme Court.

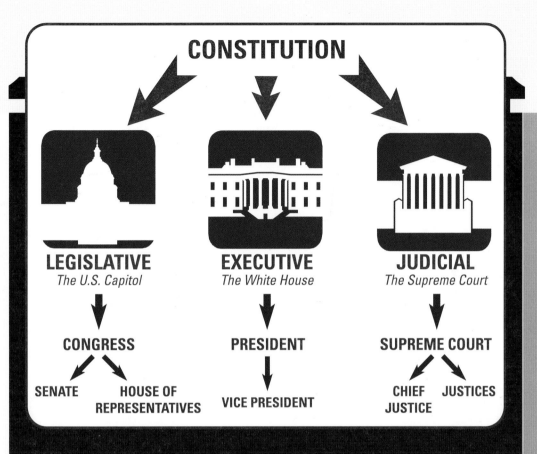

CONSTITUTION

LEGISLATIVE
The U.S. Capitol

EXECUTIVE
The White House

JUDICIAL
The Supreme Court

CONGRESS

PRESIDENT

SUPREME COURT

SENATE **HOUSE OF REPRESENTATIVES**

VICE PRESIDENT

CHIEF JUSTICE **JUSTICES**

each other's powers. The Supreme Court members are appointed for life. However, if they do something unlawful, they may be **impeached** by the House and removed from office by the Senate.

The Supreme Court's main task is to interpret the laws of our nation. Supreme Court justices study what a law says and decide if it agrees with the Constitution. Thousands of cases are presented to the Court each year, but it only has time for a few of them. The justices decide to hear and rule on the cases that have the greatest effect on the lives of American citizens.

Texas

Alaska

California

CALIFORNIA REPUBLIC

State Governments

The term "**federalism**" describes how power is shared between federal and state governments. The states and the country have duties that are alike, such as collecting taxes, borrowing money, and writing and enforcing laws. However, they also have powers that are different. The federal government makes decisions about trade with other nations and between states. It also has the ability to declare war and coin money. The state governments are responsible for trade within the state and taking care of public health and safety. One important task of state governments is **ratifying** amendments to the U.S. Constitution.

Every state has its own constitution that's similar to the U.S. Constitution. The individual state constitutions are very much like the national one, but important differences exist between them. The primary difference is that laws made at the state level can't disagree with laws made at the national level. The laws of the U.S. Constitution always come first. A state constitution addresses many

Just as the U.S. flag is a symbol of the United States, state flags, like those shown here, are symbols of the states they represent.

different items, including when it became a state, where in America it is located, and what ideas it has about the way to properly govern itself.

The Legislative Branch of State Government

Most state governments have a legislative branch called the legislature. Like Congress, it has two parts—a senate and a house or assembly. It's important to know that no two state governments are exactly alike, but most of them resemble the federal government in how they operate. State laws can be proposed in either house of the legislature. These laws can't go against the U.S. Constitution.

The legislative branch in a state government is responsible for giving funds to government **agencies** and deciding how to help local governments. States have to balance the needs of big cities and small towns, particularly in the case of large states like California or New York. The legislature must be able to represent all the state's citizens and not simply a small section of the population.

A state's legislative branch tries to make laws that are fair for everyone. This includes people who live in rural areas, those who live in suburban areas, and those who live in urban areas.

rural

suburban

urban

The Executive Branch of State Government

The person in charge of a state government's executive branch is called the governor. This person is similar to the president of the United States. A governor enforces state laws, but also has other duties, including appointing state employees and helping pass state **budgets**. The governor doesn't have total control over the state government. Power is shared using the same system of checks and balances that exists in the federal government.

A governor's main responsibility is enforcing state law. Problems have occurred in the past when governors and presidents have had different ideas of how to enforce the law. When the Civil Rights Act was passed in 1964, some states didn't want blacks and whites to live equally. President Lyndon B. Johnson used his higher authority to enforce the laws some governors didn't want to enforce. Once again, this is because the power of the state can't be greater than the power of the federal government. The U.S. Constitution is

Arnold Schwarzenegger stands with his wife, Maria Shriver, as he is sworn in as governor of California. The people of a state elect the governor, who usually serves a 4-year term.

the supreme law of the land and must be enforced ahead of any state constitution or law.

The Judicial Branch of State Government

No two state judicial systems are exactly alike. However, there are similarities between them. Most state court systems are made up of two different kinds of courts. Legal cases are first heard in trial courts. A court of appeals can review your case if you think your trial didn't follow the law. The highest state court is the state's version of the Supreme Court. Voters elect state judges, who serve for a fixed number of years. The number of years varies from state to state.

Judges in state courts need to interpret established laws in order to make decisions. However, the decisions they make can influence state laws particularly when they believe a law is outdated or incorrect. State courts have a limited area of **jurisdiction**. That means their rulings can be changed by a greater authority. The U.S.

On November 20, 2000, the Florida Supreme Court listened to arguments pertaining to a recounting of votes that had been cast in Florida during the 2000 presidential election.

Supreme Court in Washington, D.C., handles cases that involve constitutional issues when there are disagreements regarding the decisions made by the state courts.

Local Governments

Local governments follow the same pattern as the state and federal models. There is separation of powers, with legislative, executive, and judicial branches. The government offices and agencies near where you live provide you with more immediate services. They're just as important as governments at the state and federal levels. There are some situations when the federal, state, and local governments all have to work together to help people. We often see this when a natural disaster happens, such as a hurricane or an earthquake.

There's more than one type or level of local government. A county is the largest **administrative** division of a U.S. state. For example, New York State has 62 counties. Buffalo, New York, is Erie County's largest city and its administrative center. A township (often shortened to "town") is a part of a county that's run by a local government. A **municipality** is a city, town, or other district with its own local government. A special district, such as a hospital or

> Buffalo City Hall, shown here, is the seat of government for the city of Buffalo, New York.

college, gives specialized services only to the people who live in them. A school district administers the schools in a particular area.

The Legislative Branch of Local Government

A local government's legislative branch has the task of making laws just like the legislative branches at the state and national levels. Different names may be used for the legislative bodies in the thousands of local governments across our country. However, the services they provide are quite similar. A county legislature is a group of elected representatives who make laws for the county. A Supreme Court ruling in 1968 said that all legislative districts within a county had to be close in population. Some districts are made up of multiple but sparsely populated counties. Others are small sections of densely populated counties. This was done so that everyone would be equally represented in their local government.

The legislative body of a city is often called a city council. City councils deal with the special needs of urban areas. Over three-quarters of the U.S. population now live in cities. Areas with

City councils often hold public meetings like this one to find out what the people they govern think.

greater populations often have more crime, pollution, and traffic.

The legislative body of a town is often called a town council. One issue many towns face is attracting more businesses. Having more businesses means having more jobs and economic success.

The Executive Branch of Local Government

The executive branch of county government is often led by a county executive; some counties are run by a board of executives. It's their job to enforce laws. The county executive could be considered the president of a county. However, they certainly don't have presidential powers, such as the control of the military or the authority to meet with leaders of other countries. The county executive can veto decisions made by a county legislature and is in charge of all the departments in a county's government.

A mayor is the elected official who is usually in charge of a municipal government (although some municipalities hire a town or city manager). The mayor must represent the needs of all the people in a city or town. A mayor, like a county executive, is most often elected to a 4-year term. A mayor's duties may include enforcing laws, appointing city employees, and leading the community through local emergencies.

In August 2008, New Orleans mayor Ray Nagin (center) and members of city government held a press conference to warn local citizens about Tropical Storm Gustav.

governor

- in charge of the executive branch of a state government

- duties include: appointing some state employees and helping pass state budgets

mayor

- in charge of the executive branch of a municipal (local) government

- duties include: appointing some city employees and submitting budgets to the city council

enforces the law

president

- represents the United States around the world

- in charge of the executive branch of the federal government

- leader of the U.S. military

The executive office of a town government may be a town supervisor, an elected mayor, or a hired manager. The supervisor's duties are often very similar to a mayor's. However, the supervisor works with a town council as opposed to a city council.

The Judicial Branch of Local Government

Courts at the local level vary from state to state and even county to county. A city court tries people accused of breaking municipal laws. A town court tries people who are accused of breaking town laws. Cases involving more serious crimes, such as kidnapping, are handled at the state and federal levels.

City and town courts have control over a large number of matters relating to the U.S. justice system. Automobile and traffic matters are handled by local courts. If someone gets a speeding ticket or does something else that's against the rules of the road, they go to a local court. Small claims issues handled by local courts are cases

The city courts of many small cities are located in the city hall, like this one. Larger cities often have separate buildings for their local courts.

between local citizens that usually concern amounts under $5,000 in most states. Evictions are handled in local courts, too. An eviction is when a business or individual is forced to move out of an office or home for failure to pay the rent.

Serving the Public

Our nation's government is divided into three different levels, each with three different branches. It has been set up so that one branch doesn't have more power than any other. The legislative, executive, and judicial branches all have their roles to play in making a government that serves the people in the best manner possible. We're very fortunate to be living in a country that struggles to preserve our rights at the federal, state, and local levels.

While the U.S. government is run by many kinds of politicians, it's American citizens who choose the politicians who make, enforce, and interpret the laws that make our country a great place to live. It's your great challenge and honor as an American to vote for U.S. politicians when you turn 18. It takes responsible voters to elect responsible politicians.

Glossary

administrative (uhd-MIH-nuh-stray-tihv) Having to do with the management or organization of a group's affairs.

agency (AY-juhn-see) A special department of the government.

Articles of Confederation (AHR-tih-kuhlz UV kuhn-feh-duh-RAY-shun) The laws that governed the United States before the Constitution was created.

budget (BUH-jiht) A plan for how to spend a certain amount of money over a period of time.

executive (ihg-ZEH-kyuh-tihv) Having to do with the branch of government that enforces laws.

federalism (FEH-duh-ruh-lih-zuhm) The division of power between a central government and regional governments.

impeach (ihm-PEECH) To accuse an official of misconduct while in office.

judicial (joo-DIH-shul) Having to do with the branch of government that explains the meanings of laws and tries cases.

jurisdiction (juhr-uhs-DIHK-shun) The area over which legal authority extends.

legislative (LEH-juhs-lay-tihv) Having to do with the branch of government that makes laws.

monarchy (MAH-nuhr-kee) A government run by a king or queen.

municipality (myoo-nih-suh-PAA-luh-tee) A city, town, or other region that has its own government.

ratify (RA-tuh-fy) To approve or agree to something in an official way.

representative (reh-prih-ZEHN-tuh-tihv) A person chosen to speak for others.

U.S. Constitution (YOO EHS kahn-stuh-TOO-shun) The document adopted in 1788 that explains the different parts of the nation's government and how each part works.

Index

A
Articles of
	Confederation, 7
assembly, 16

B
balance(s), 7, 9, 16, 19

C
check(s), 7, 8, 9, 10, 12,
	19
chief justice, 12, 13
city council, 24, 27, 28
Congress, 8, 9, 10, 11,
	13, 16
Constitution, 7, 8, 10,
	11, 12, 13, 15, 16
county(ies), 23, 24, 26,
	28
county executive, 26
court(s), 20, 21, 28, 29

E
executive, 5, 10, 13, 19,
	23, 26, 27, 28, 30

F
federal, 5, 7, 8, 12, 15,
	16, 19, 27
federalism, 15

G
governor(s), 19, 27

H
house, 16
House of Representatives,
	8, 11, 13

J
judicial, 5, 12, 13, 20,
	23, 30

L
legislative, 5, 8, 13, 16,
	23, 24, 25, 30
legislature, 16, 24, 26
local, 5, 16, 23, 24, 27,
	28, 29, 30

M
manager, 26, 28
mayor, 26, 27, 28
municipal, 26, 27, 28
municipality(ies), 23, 26

N
nation(s), 7, 10, 13, 15,
	30
national, 15, 24

P
president(s), 8, 9, 10,
	11, 12, 13, 19,
	26, 27

S
senate, 16
Senate, 8, 11, 12, 13
separation of powers, 8,
	23
state(s), 5, 7, 15, 16, 19,
	20, 21, 23, 24,
	27, 28, 29, 30
supervisor, 28
Supreme Court, 12, 13,
	20, 21, 24

T
town council, 25, 28
township, 23

V
veto, 8, 9, 10, 26
vice president, 11, 13

Due to the changing nature of Internet links, The Rosen Publishing Group, Inc., has developed an online list of Web sites related to the subject of this book. This site is updated regularly. Please use this link to access the list: http://www.rcbmlinks.com/rlr/branch